Rowdy Ronnie

A Children's Book About Developing Patience and Kindness

WRITTEN BY SHERMAINE PERRY-KNIGHTS
ILLUSTRATED BY ELENA KISENKOVA

Copyright © 2023 by Innovation Consultants of DeKalb.
Written by Shermaine Perry-Knights.
Illustrated by Elena Kisenkova.

No part of this book may be used or reproduced, distributed or transmitted in any form or by any means without the prior written permission of the publisher, except in the case of brief quotations embodied in critical reviews.

ISBN: 978-1-953518-34-7

Visit www.amazinglyshermaine.com to place bulk orders for schools or associations.

◆ DEDICATION ◆

This book is dedicated to every child that wants a pet at home.
Please be kind, loving, and patient with all fur babies.
Taking care of them is an all day job, but it is a fun one!

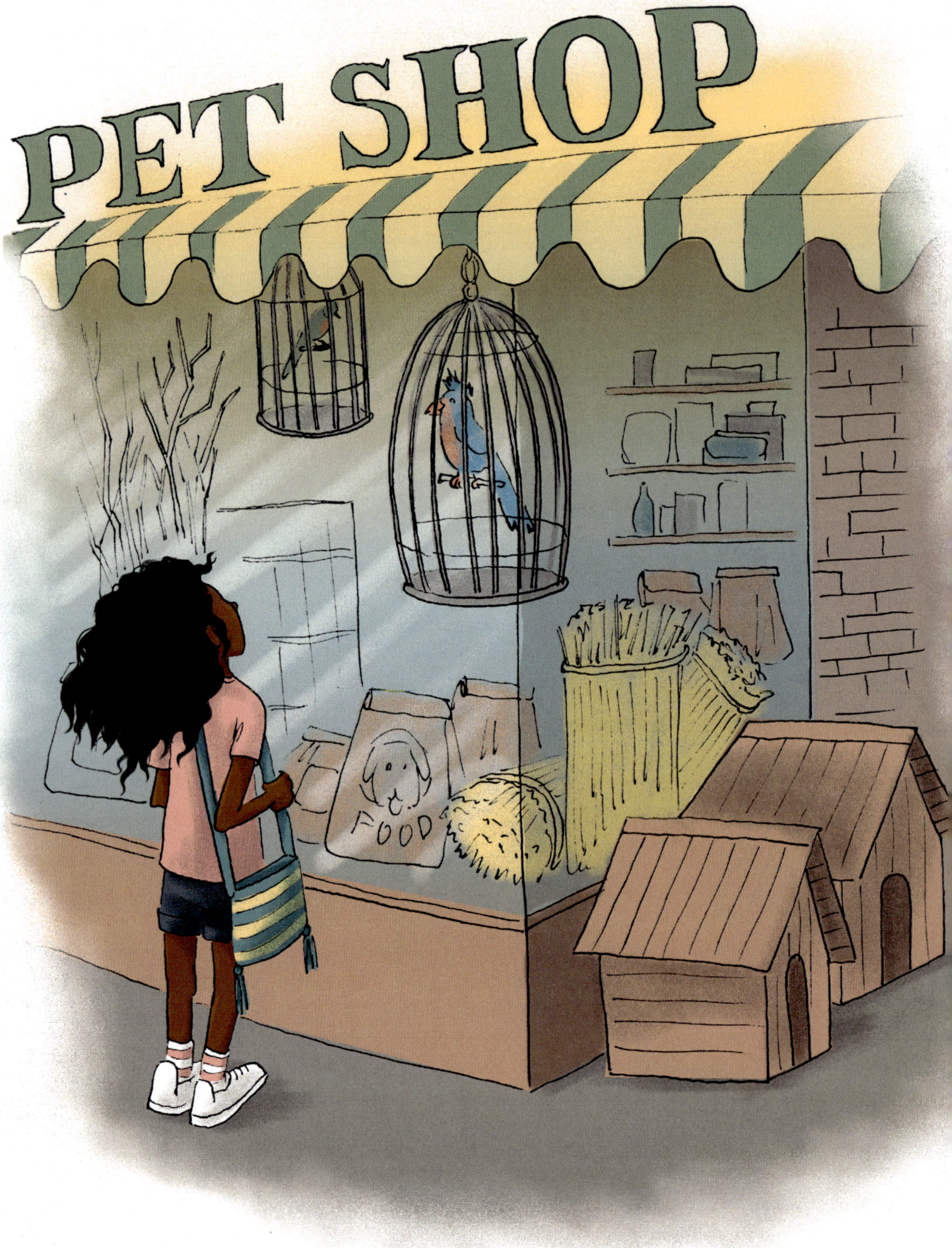
PET SHOP
FOOD

There once was a girl named Ryan.
Ryan would beg and beg her parents for a fluffy pet rabbit.

"I want a pet rabbit to cuddle and love," Ryan would say.

"I would be the best rabbit parent there ever was!"

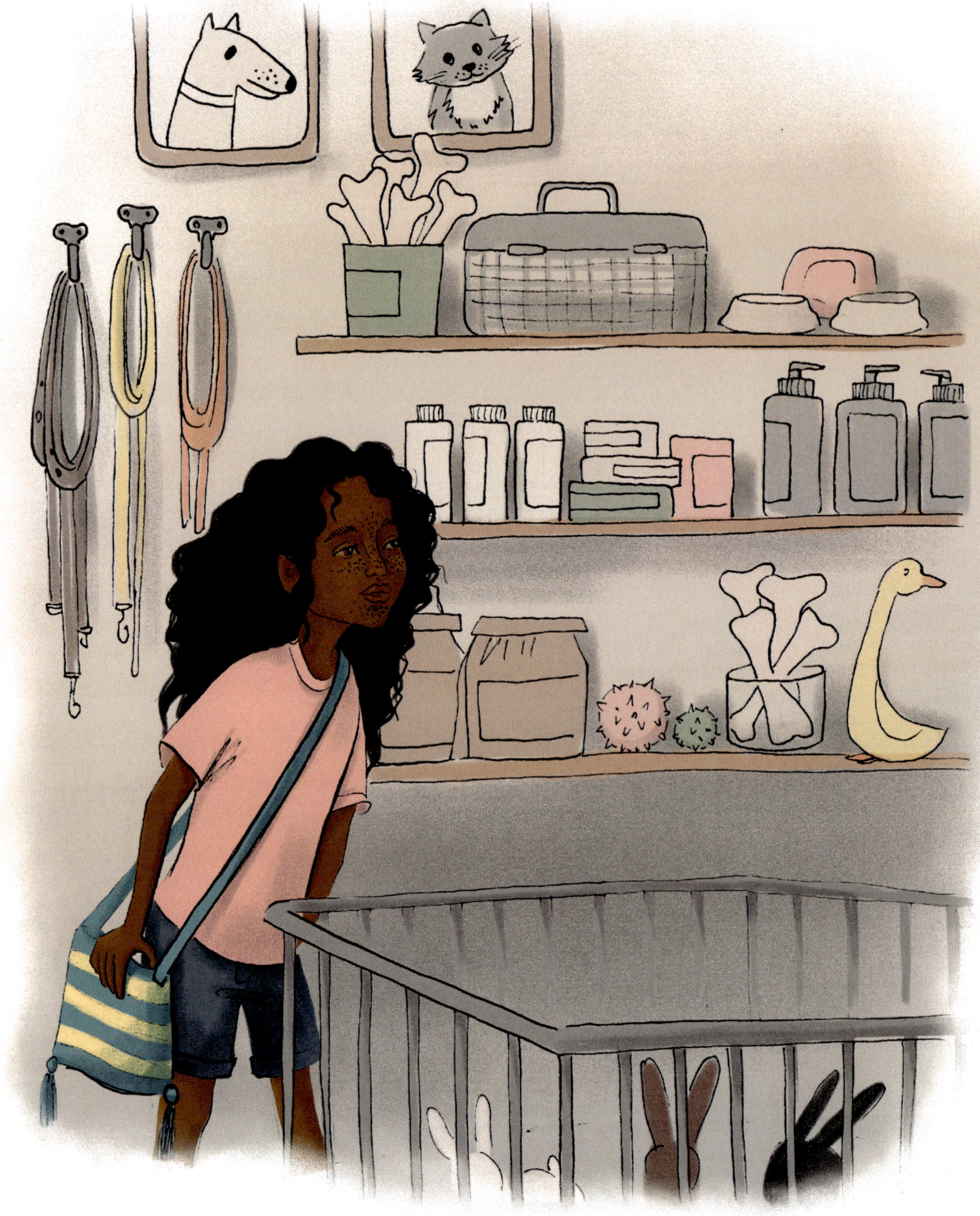

One morning, Ryan was filled with joy when her parents agreed to take her to the pet store. Ryan knew in her heart she was ready for a pet rabbit to love and care for on her own.

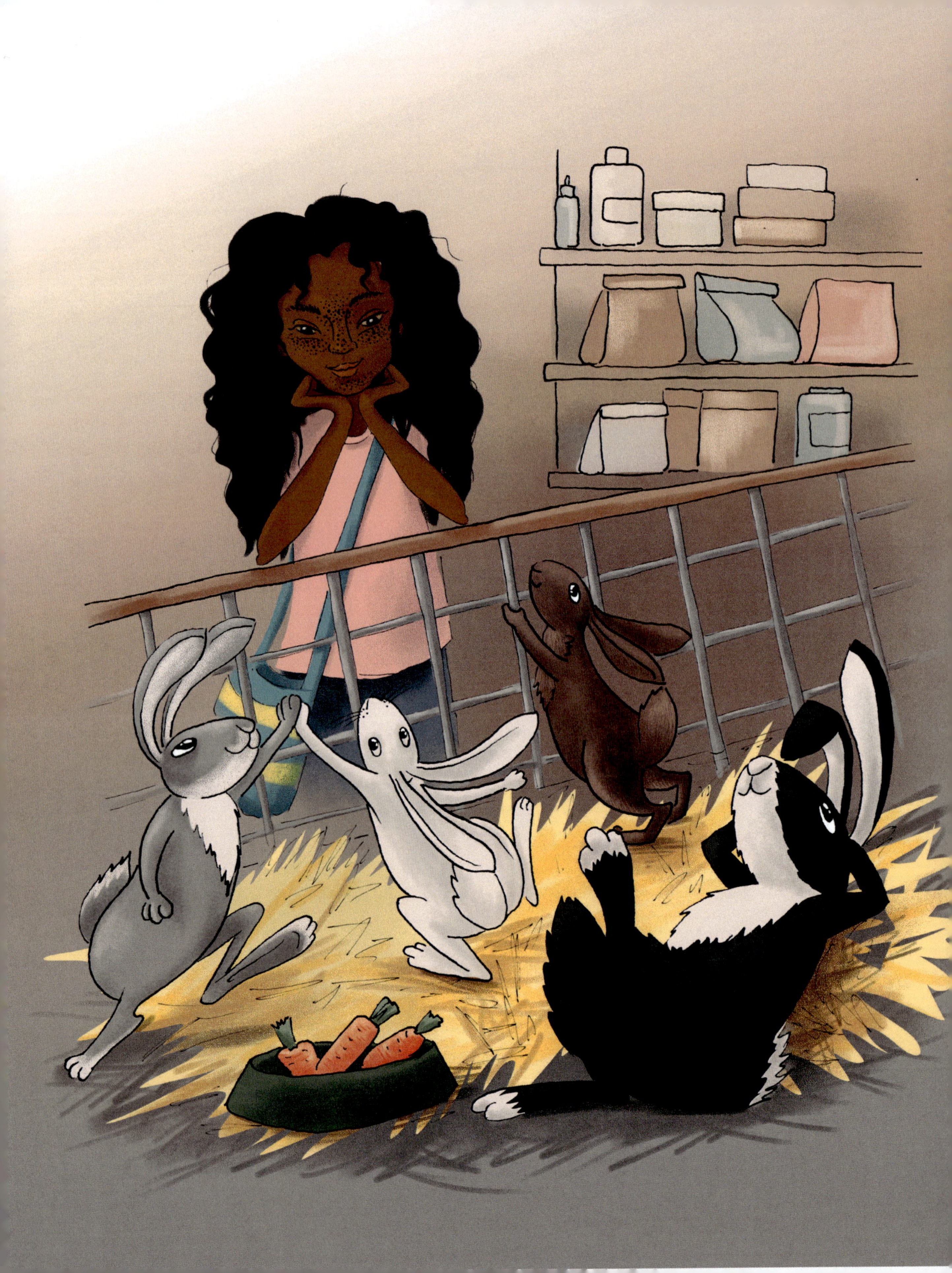

The bell rang as Ryan walked through the front door. The store was filled with happy pups barking and chirpy birds chirping.

Soon she came upon the rabbit pens.
All the rabbits began to hop when they saw Ryan.
But one black and white rabbit stayed in the back.

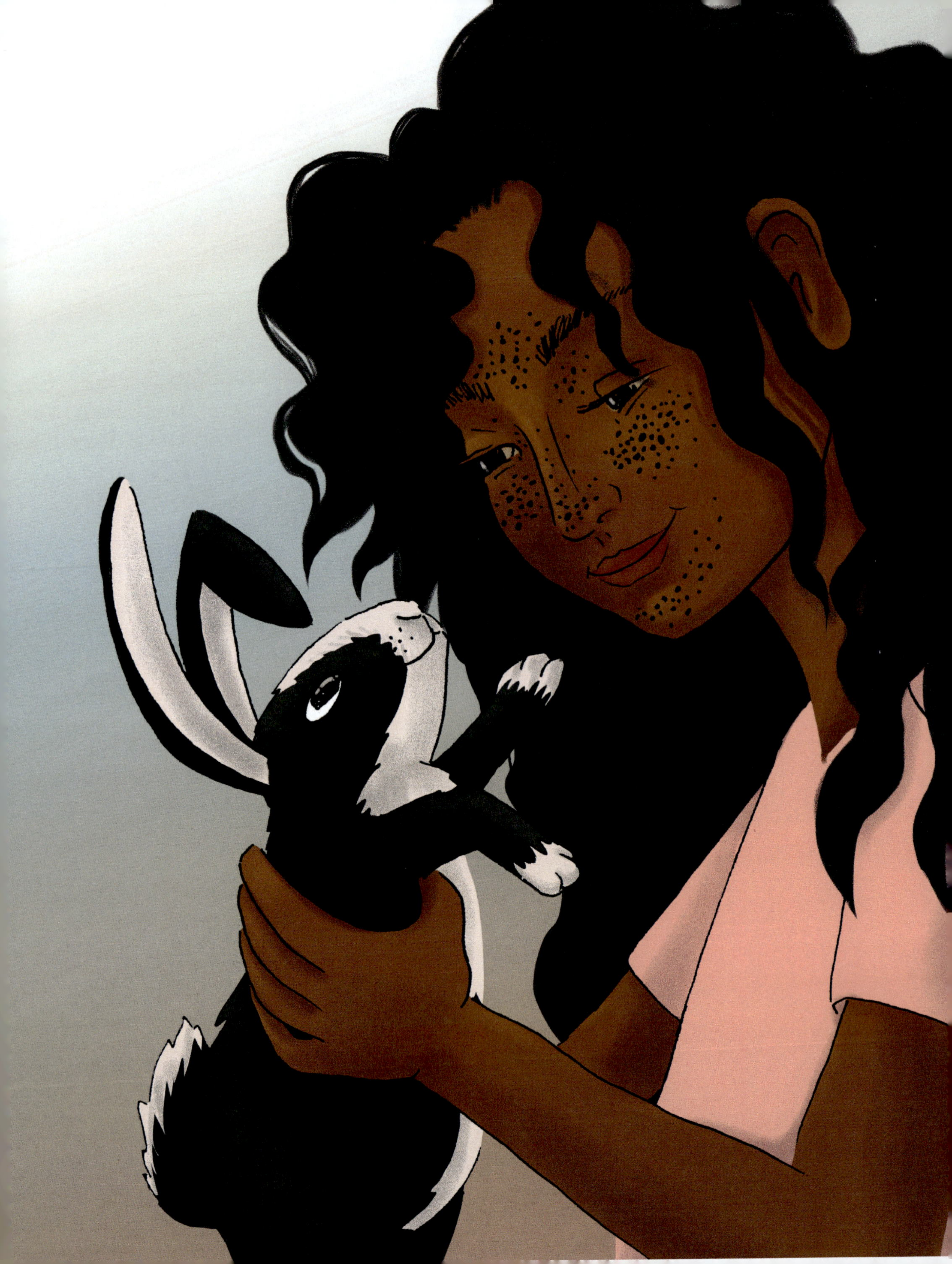

Ryan picked up the black and white rabbit and with a wiggle of the nose, the rabbit reached one paw towards her face.

This is the one! Ryan thought to herself. "I'll name you Ronnie."

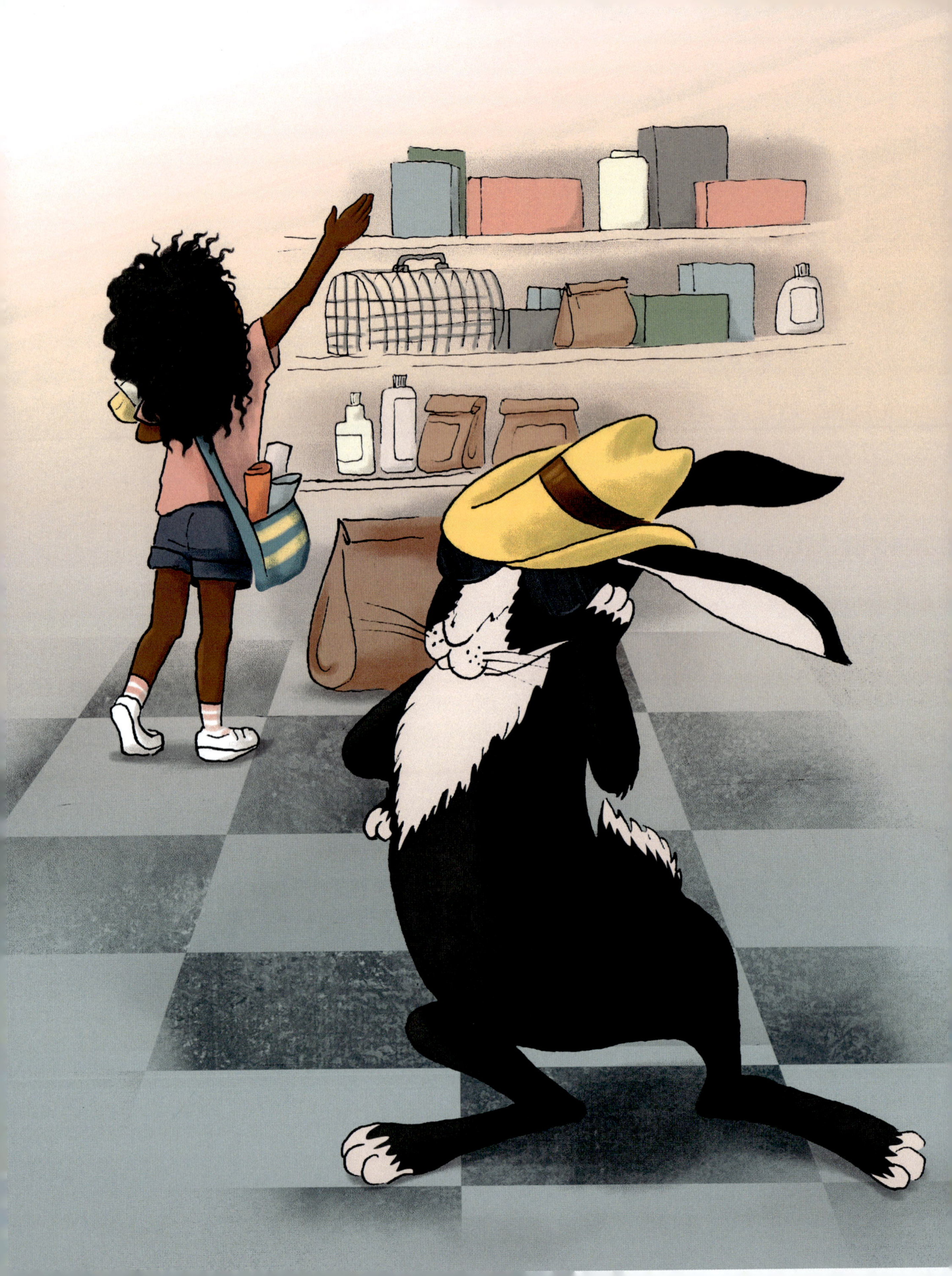

But little did Ryan know that Ronnie was the most rambunctious rabbit.

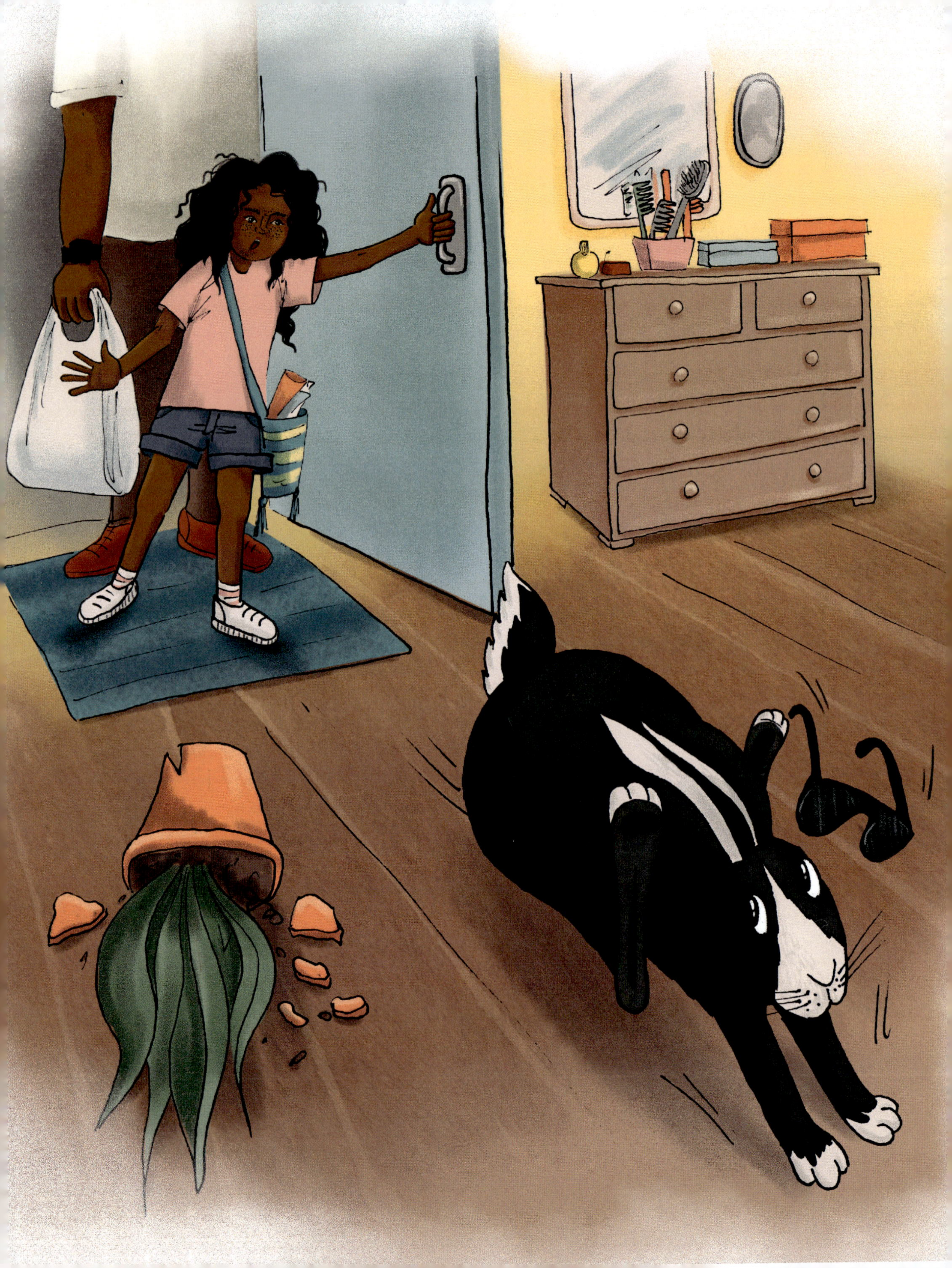

As soon as Ronnie raced through the door,
he rocked the whole house with his ruthless speed.

Knocking over pots and plants, Ryan tried to run after him,
but he was too fast with his restless racing.

"No Ronnie, nooo!" Ryan would shout.
"It seems like Ronnie will never relax!" Ryan would complain.

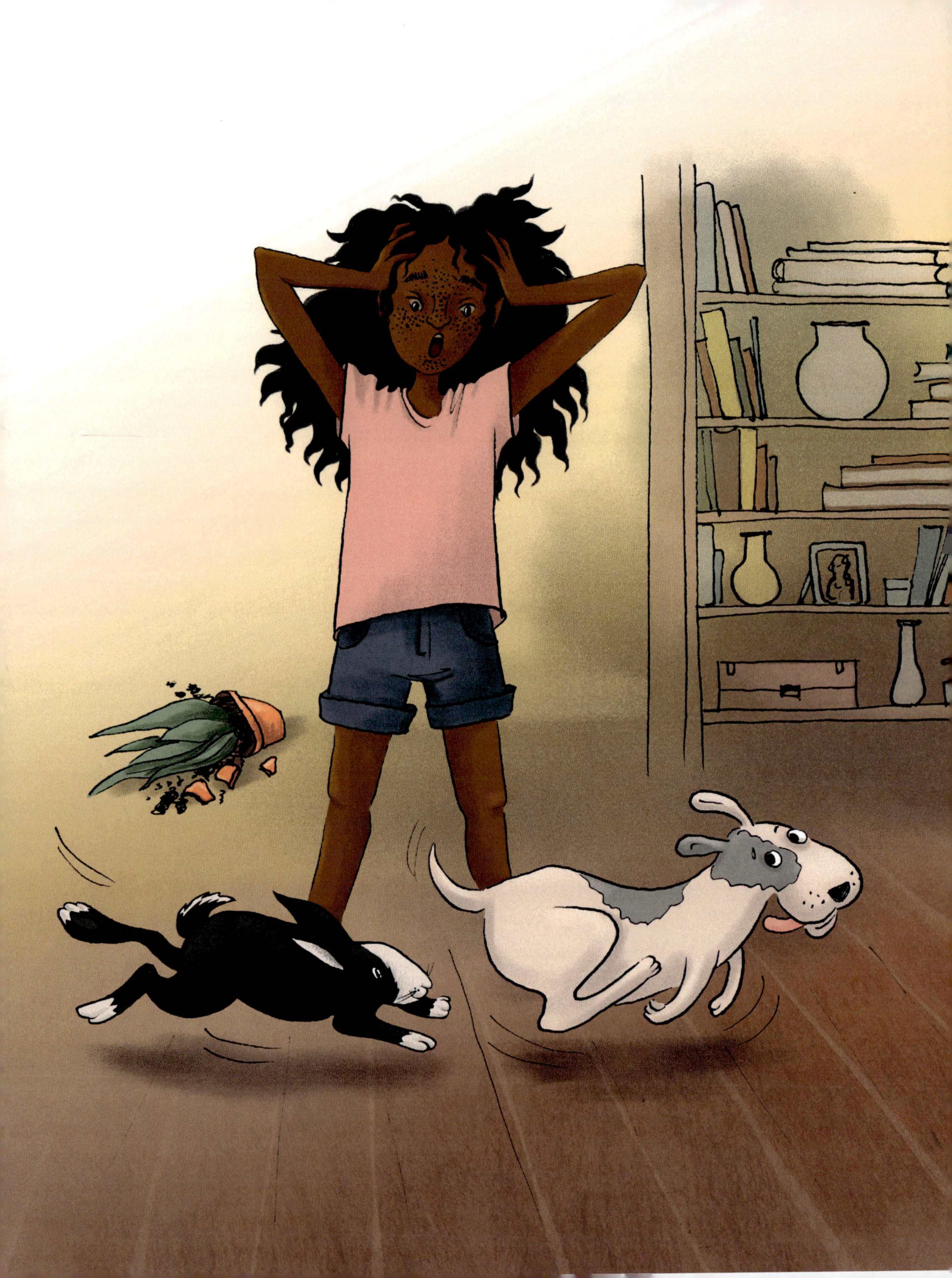

Ronnie even liked to chase Ryan's dog Rex. He would nip at his tail, and they would run around the whole complex.

"Ronnie, come back here!" Ryan would scream.
But Ronnie wouldn't listen.

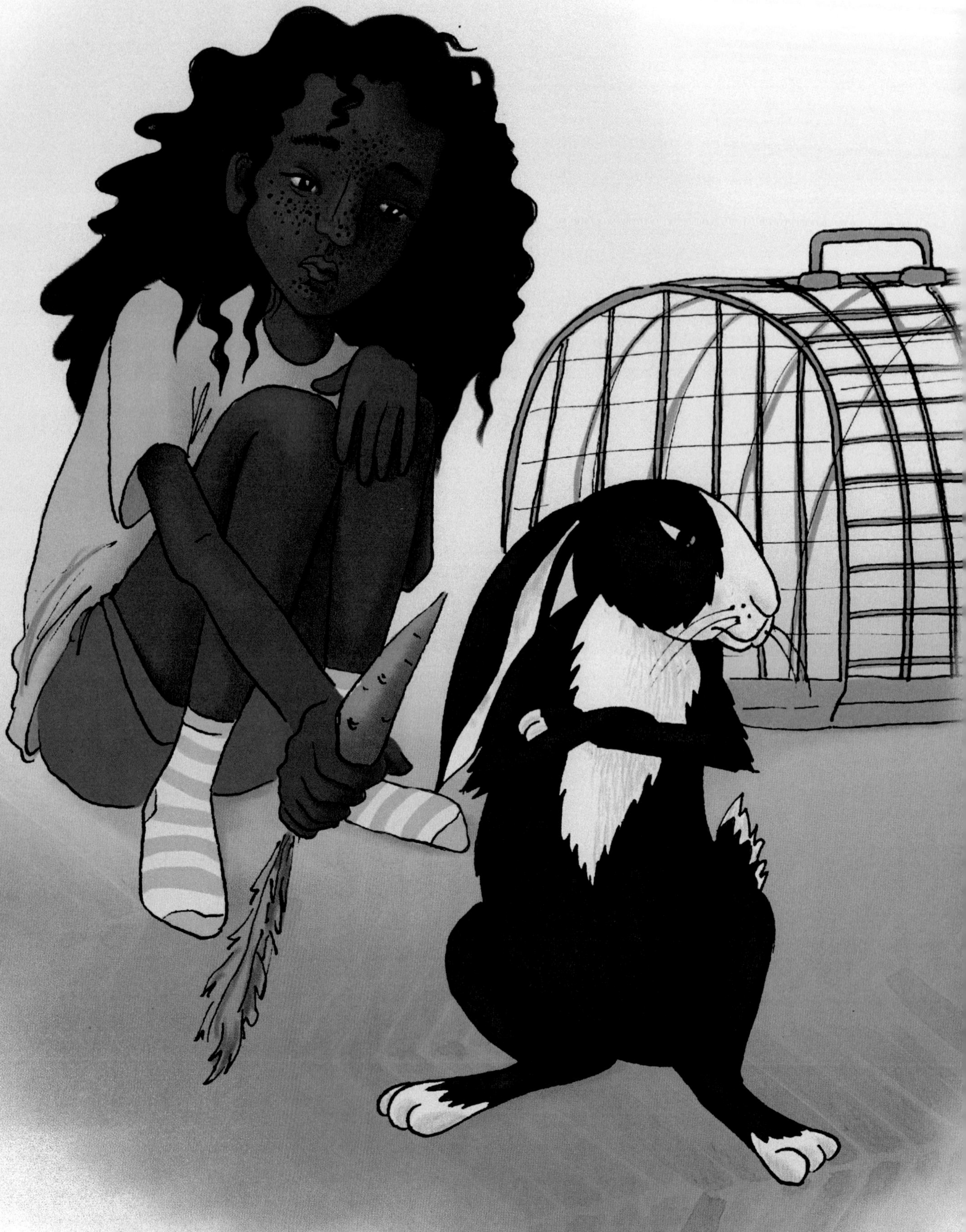

Ronnie would refuse to eat anything,
even his favorite orange carrot snack.

"C'mon on Ronnie, just one bite!" Ryan would plead.

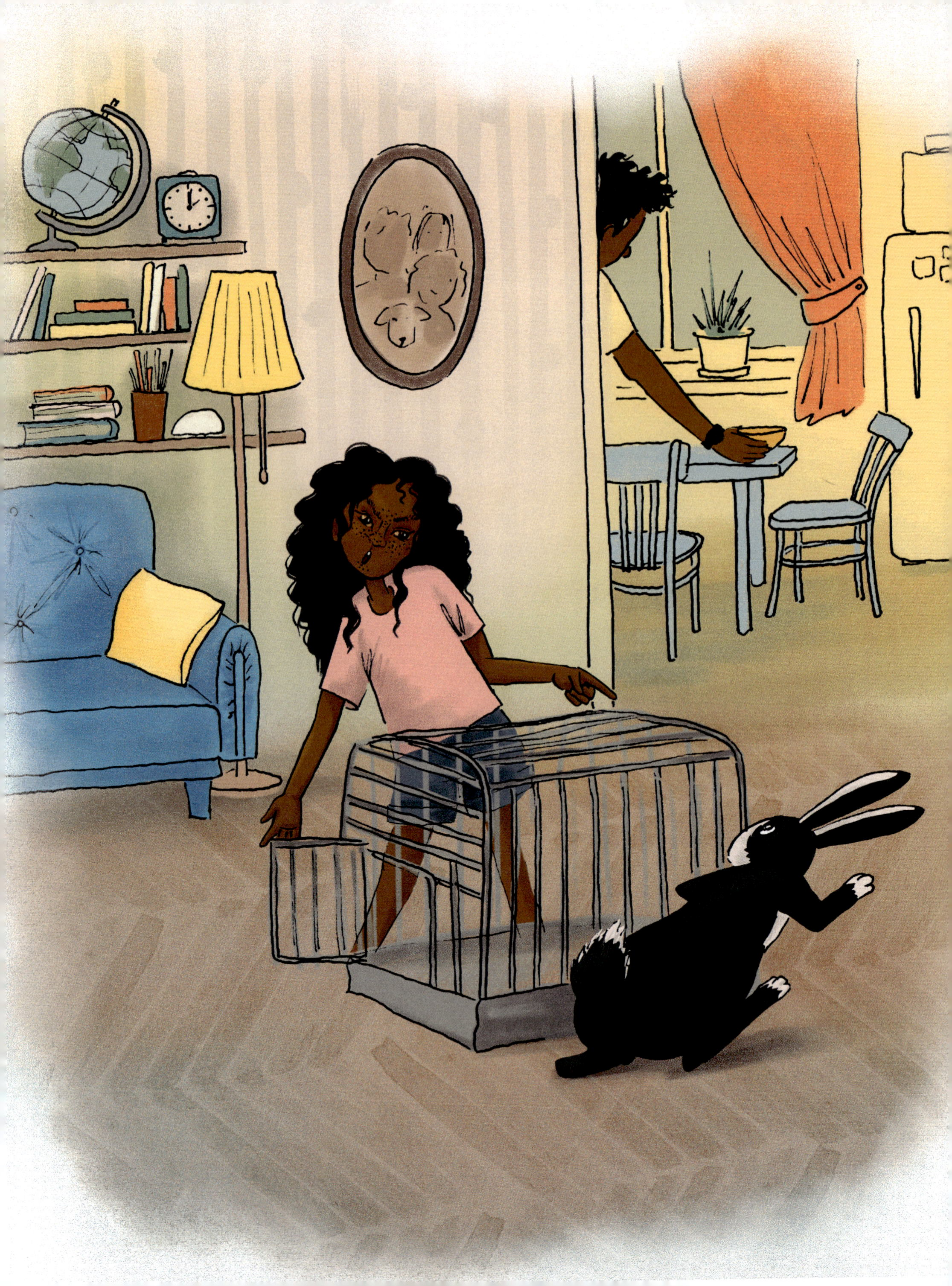

Ronnie would refuse to go into his pen.
And Ronnie refused to ever listen.

Ronnie would squeak and Ronnie would groan.
Ryan had no idea how messy Ronnie could be in her home.

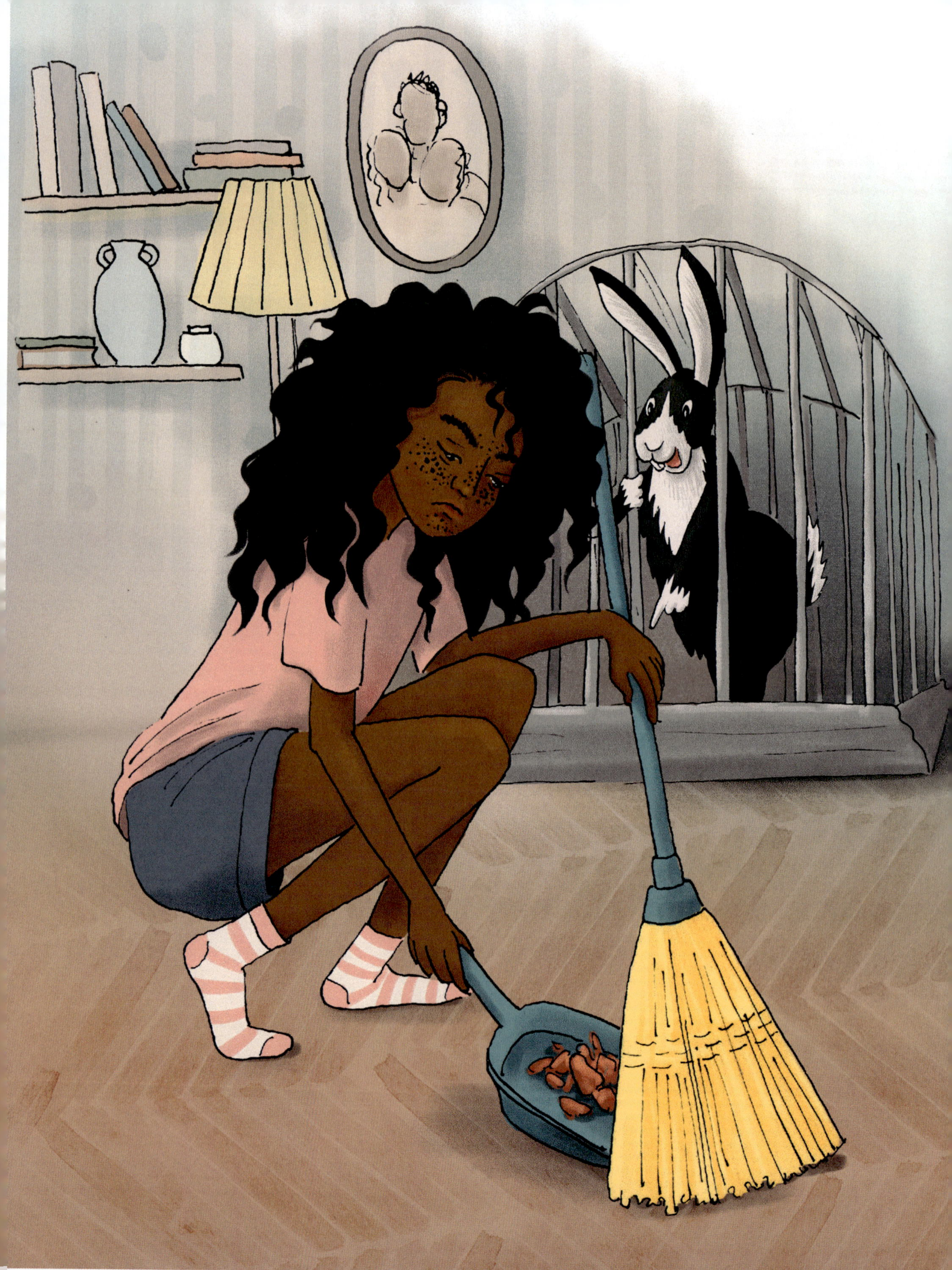

"Not again! Another mess to clean!"
Ryan would scrub the carpet and mop up the floor.

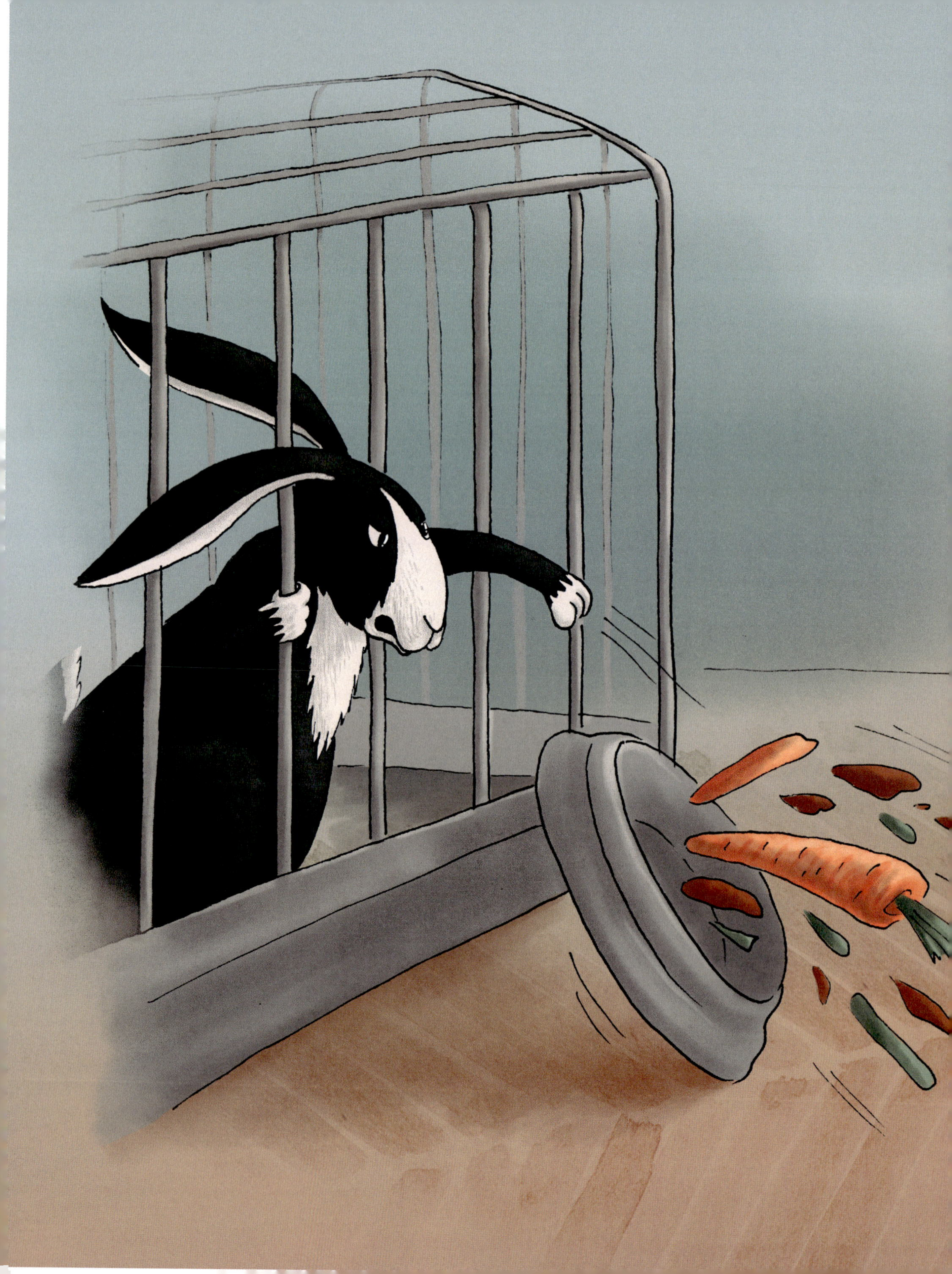

When Ronnie finally went into his cage,
he would so make so much noise, noise, noise!

Ronnie would whack his bowl all round.
And Ronnie would jump up and down, bouncing so loud.

"I can't take it anymore! I wish I never brought Ronnie home!"
Ryan would cry.

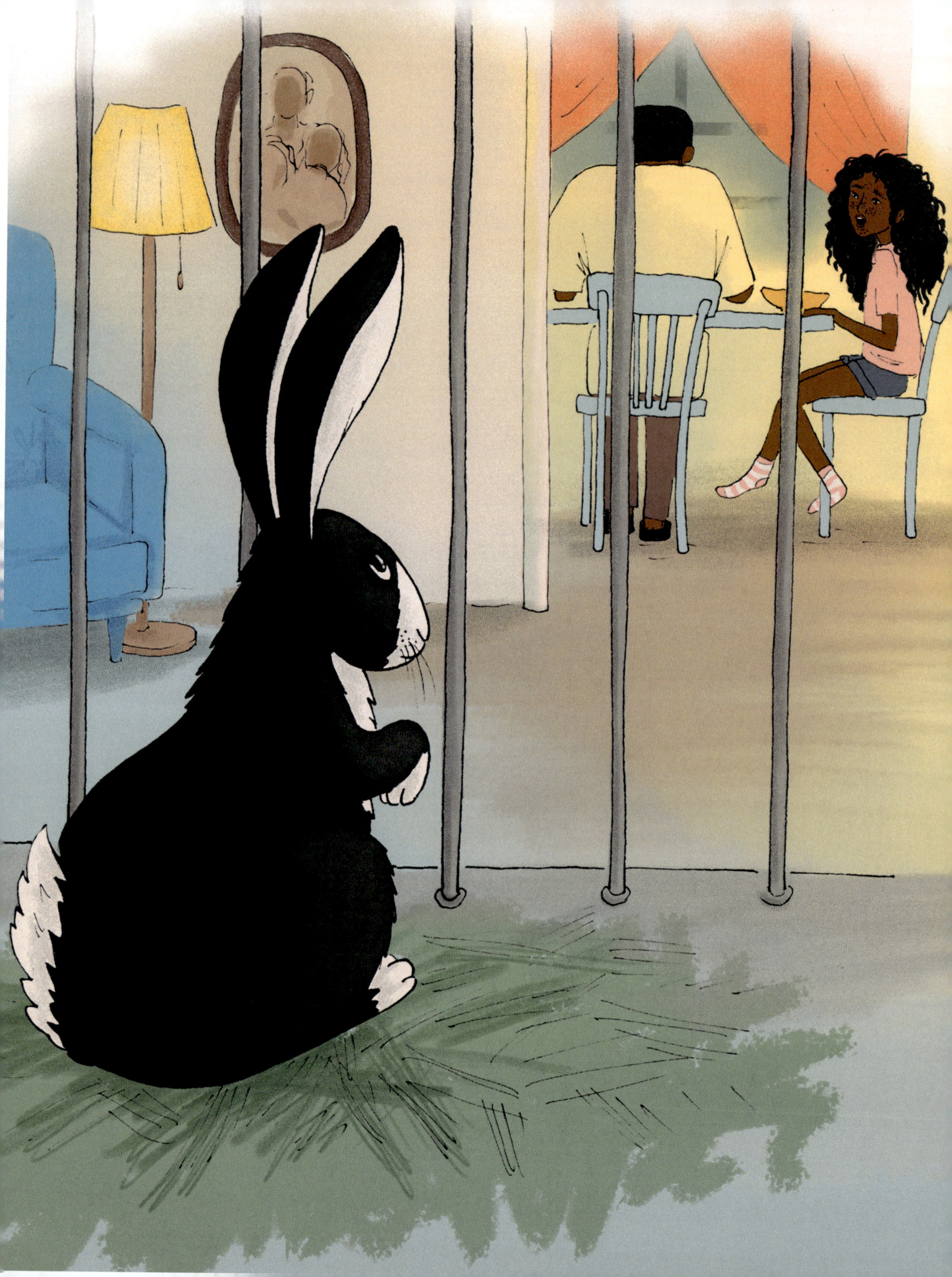

During dinner Ronnie was especially loud.

"Ronnie is the worst rabbit!"
Ryan yelled to her parents over her soup.

"He never listens to me, and sometimes I feel like Ronnie hates me." Ryan crumbled her face into her hands and tears started to run to her face.

"I wish Ronnie wasn't here." Ryan continued.

Ryan's parents listened closely, and they comforted Ryan with a hug. "Having a pet is not always easy." Ryan's mom explained.

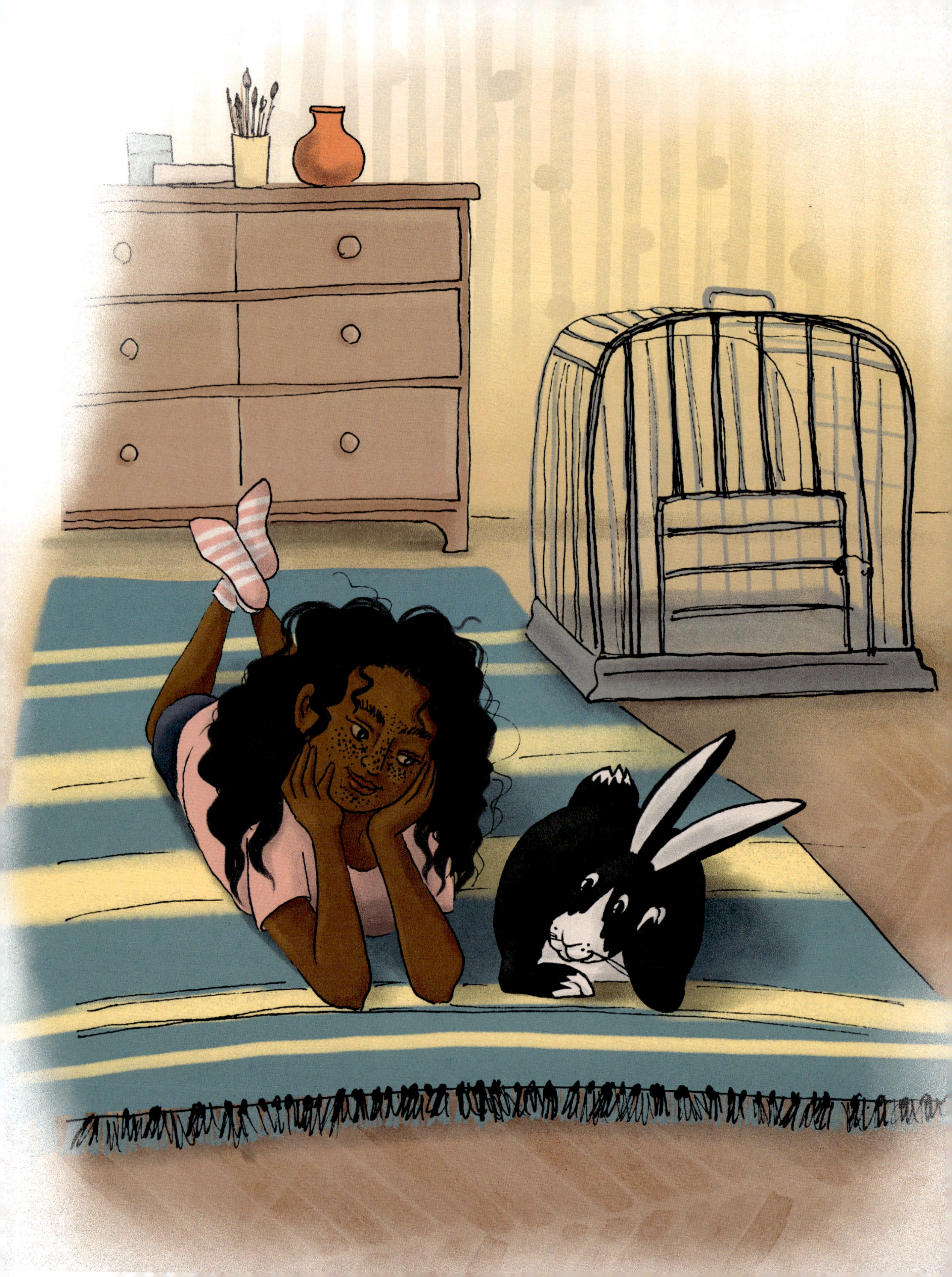

"Pets require patience and guidance. Ronnie will learn how to be good rabbit. But you need to have patience and show him the way."

For the rest of dinner, Ryan decided to ignore Ronnie's rowdy side. She sat at the kitchen table with her parents while Ronnie watched.

As soon as Ronnie relaxed Ryan showed her fluffy rabbit some love and attention. Ryan picked Ronnie up, and she snuggled him close.

Ronnie's small fluffy tail started to wag,
and he enjoyed being loved by Ryan!

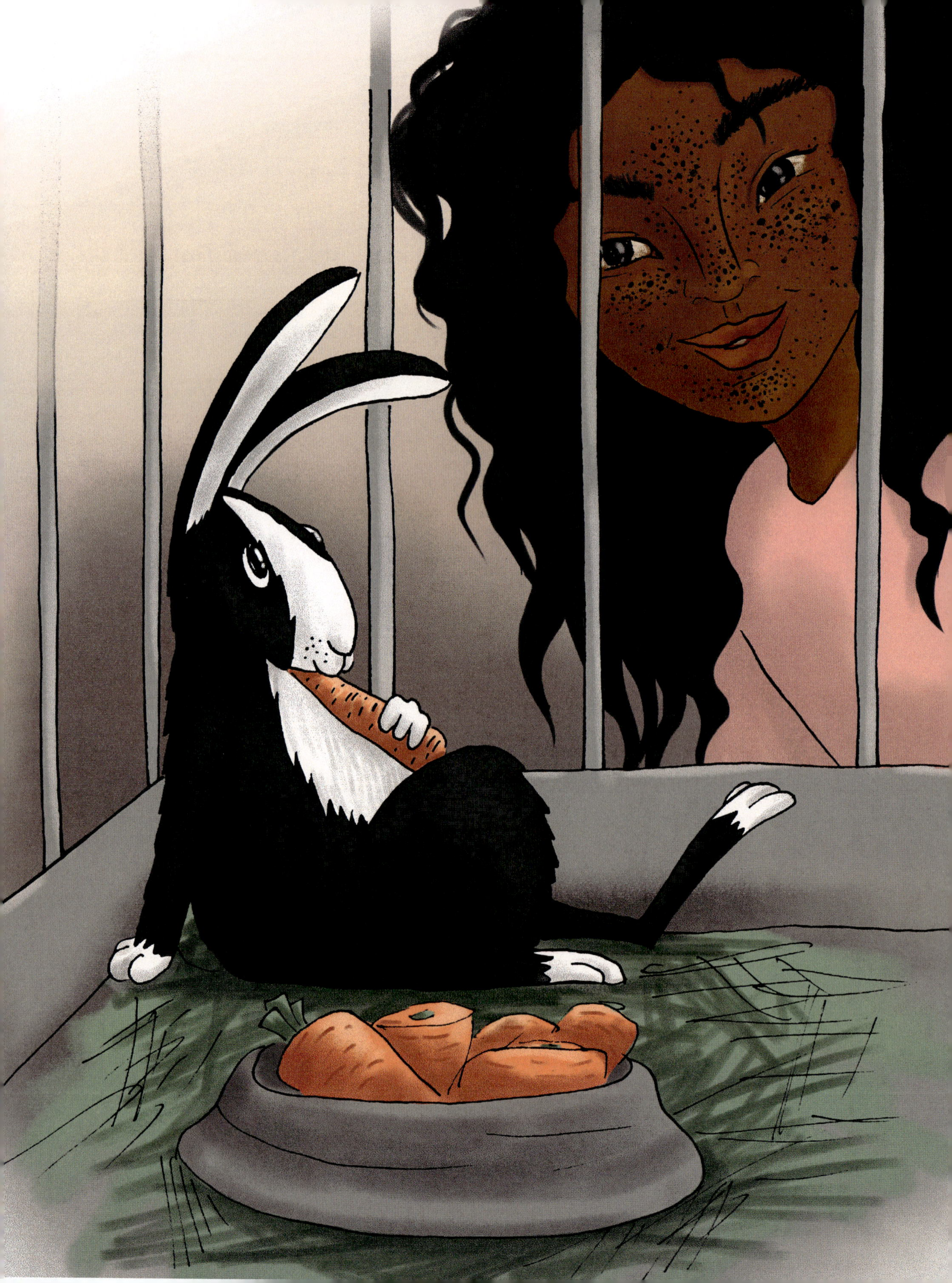

"I promise to be more patient." Ryan whispered to Ronnie.

Soon Ryan learned that it was best to reward Ronnie every time he was well behaved. She sometimes had to wait a long time, but it was worth it!

When Ronnie sat quietly in his cage, Ryan rewarded Ronnie with new play pen and toys.

Ronnie hopped all around his play pen while Ryan would laugh. When Ronnie ate all the food in his bowl, Ryan rewarded him with a special treat. "Great job, Ronnie!" Ryan would exclaim!

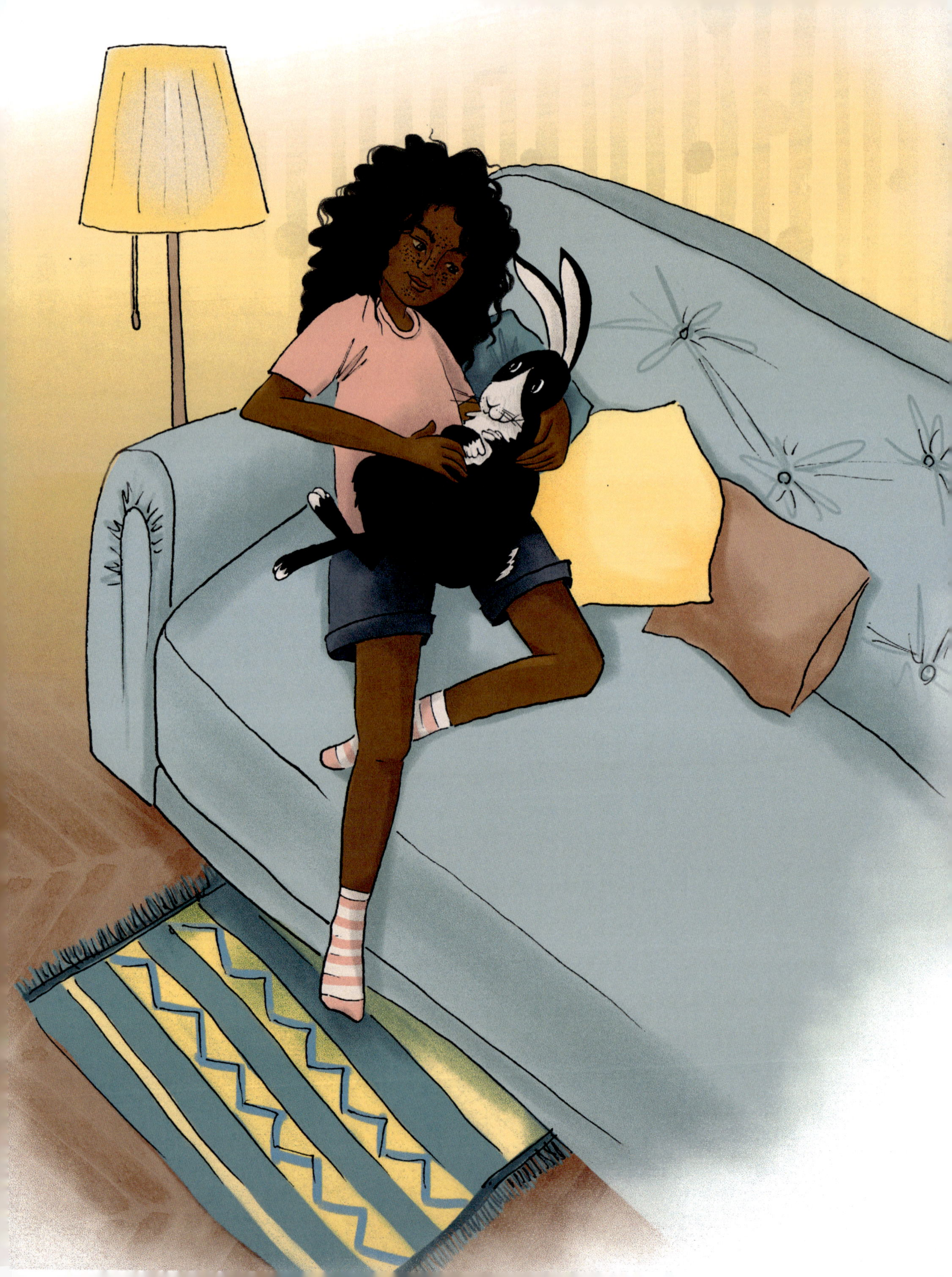

"What a good little rabbit you are," Ryan would complement.
This made Ronnie feel good.

One evening, Ryan noticed that Ronnie chewed on her favorite chair while Ryan wasn't looking. The stuffing in the chair was coming out, and the fluff was all over the floor.

Ryan took a deep breath, counted to ten in her head. She closed her eyes and smiled. Ryan swiftly moved Ronnie into his cage, and then gave him sticks that Ronnie could chew on.

"You can't chew on the furniture Ronnie, but you can chew on these carrot sticks." Ryan explained.

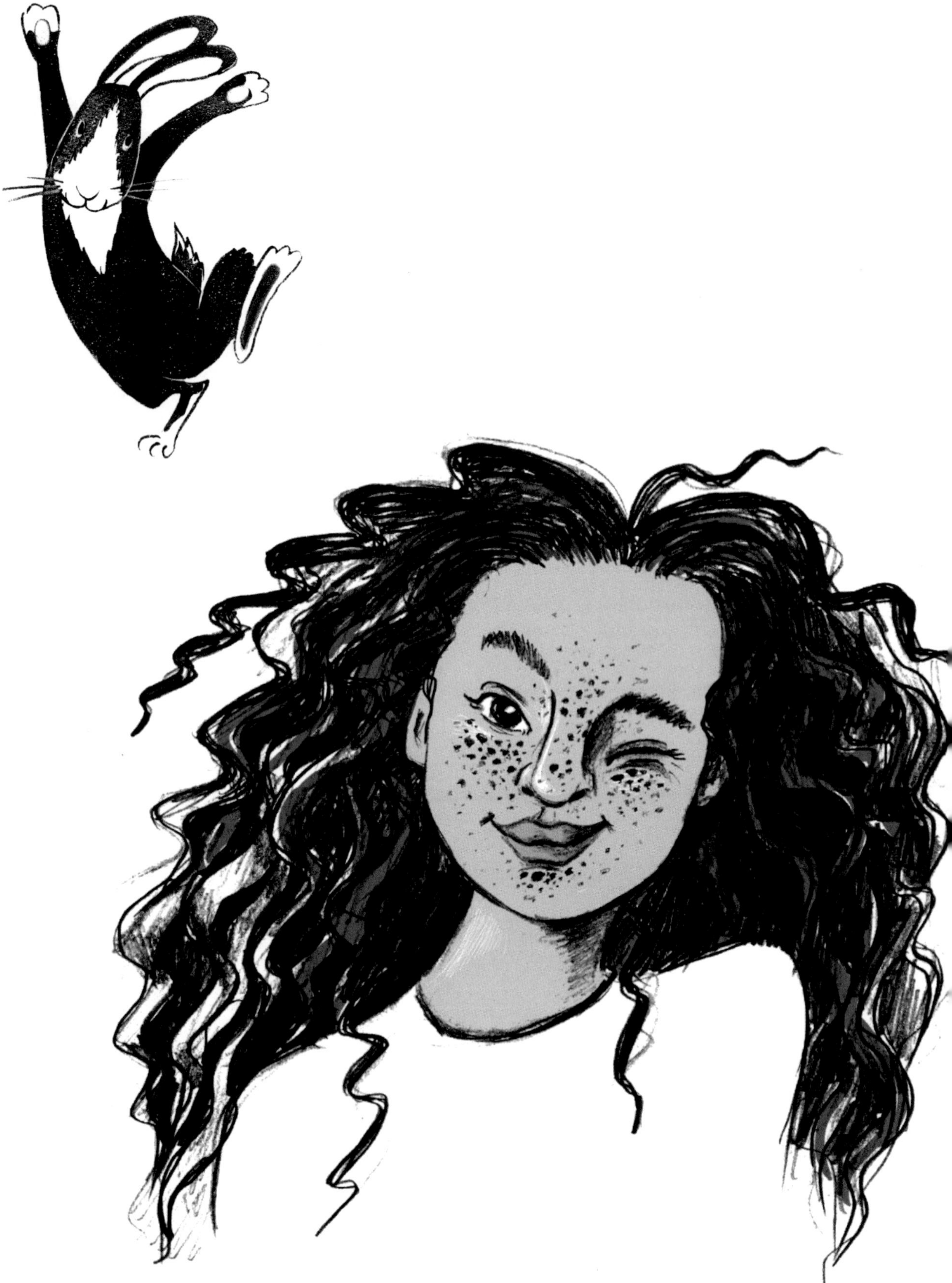

Only a few hours later, Ronnie was happily chewing on the sticks while Ryan fixed the chair with a needle and thread. Mom was nearby to lend a hand.

Ryan gave Ronnie lots of pets and snuggles for chewing on the sticks instead of the furniture.

Ronnie loved his rewards, and he loved the time he spent with Ryan. Ryan and Ronnie would relax on the bed together.

Ryan would give Ronnie lots of tasty treats.
Ryan would give Ronnie space to run and play.

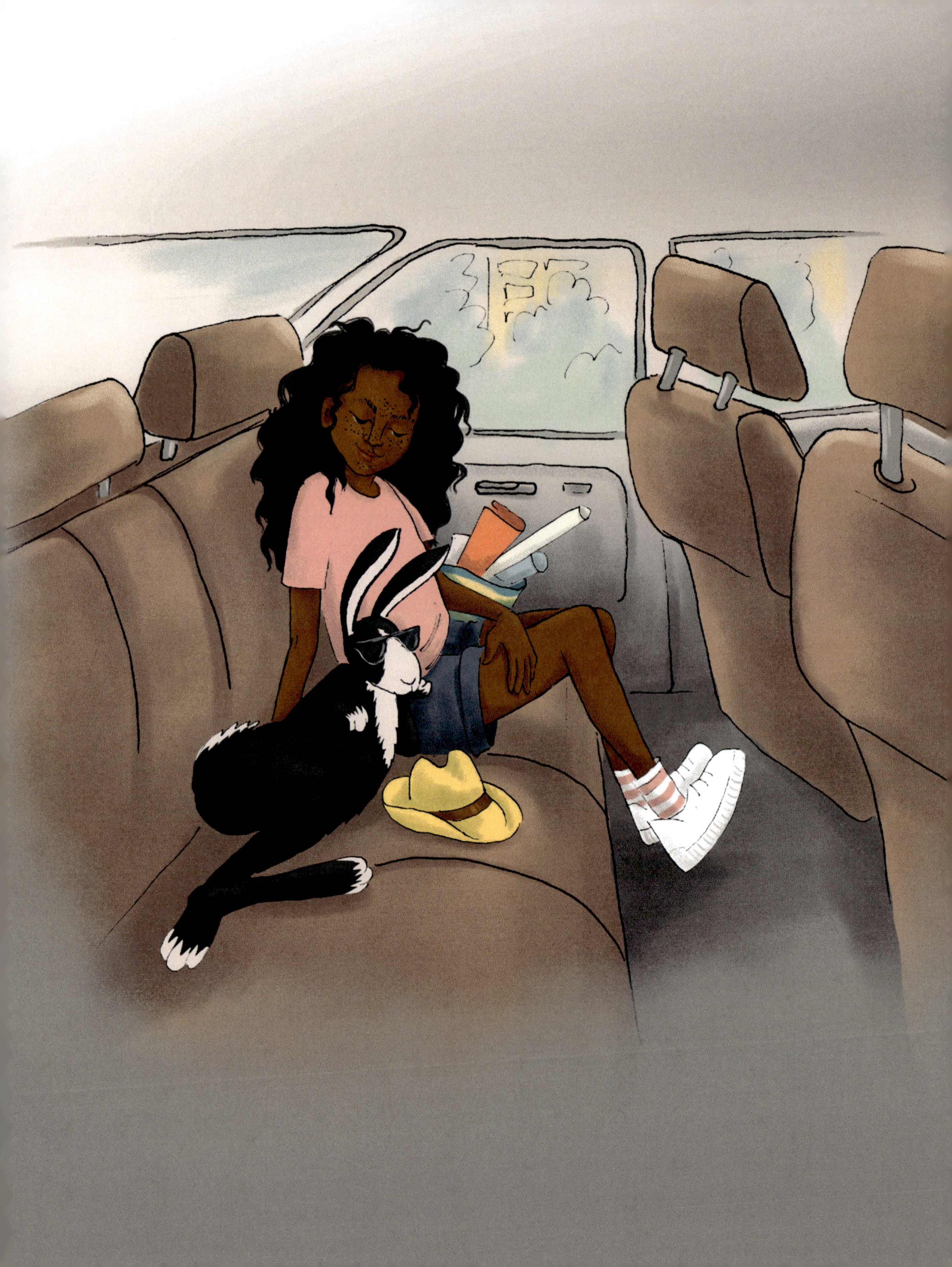

Ryan was relieved when Ronnie finally became the rabbit she always wanted.

"I love you, Ronnie!" Ryan said with a smile.
"Ronnie is the best Rabbit ever!" Ryan would say.
She decided to take him for a ride.

THE END

There's More!

AMAZINGLYSHERMAINE.COM

Scan to collect them all!

COLORING BOOKS

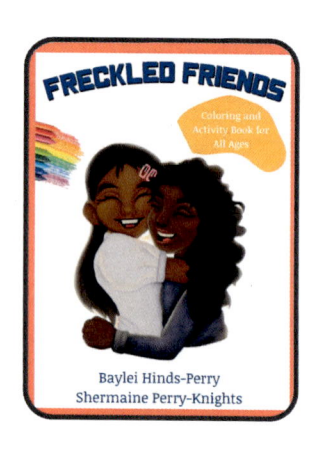

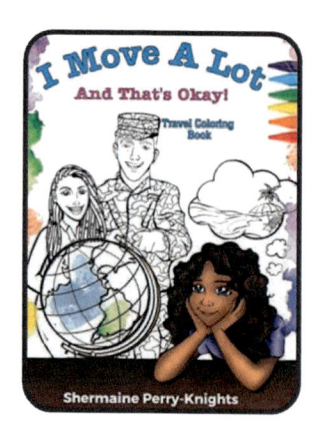

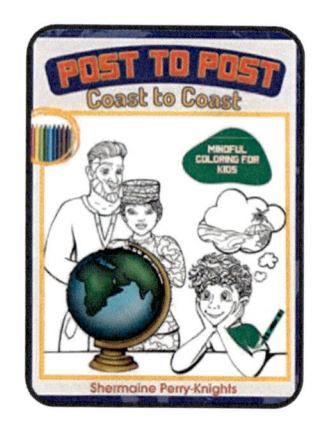

PICTURE BOOKS

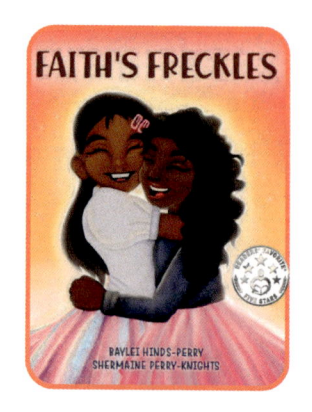

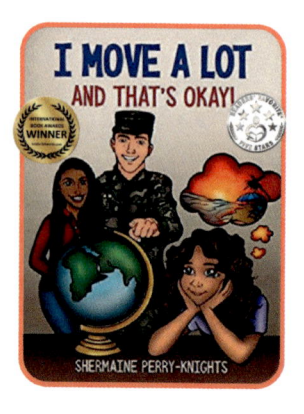

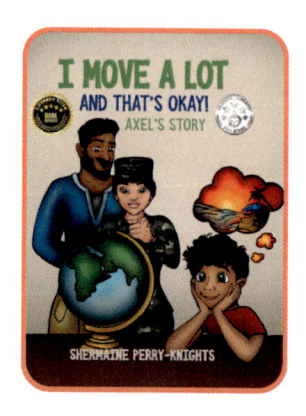

Made in the USA
Middletown, DE
02 February 2024

48892835R00022